To

I REALLY HIT THE

JACKPOT

WHEN WE BECAME FRIENDS

A WONDERFUL MEMORY OF US...

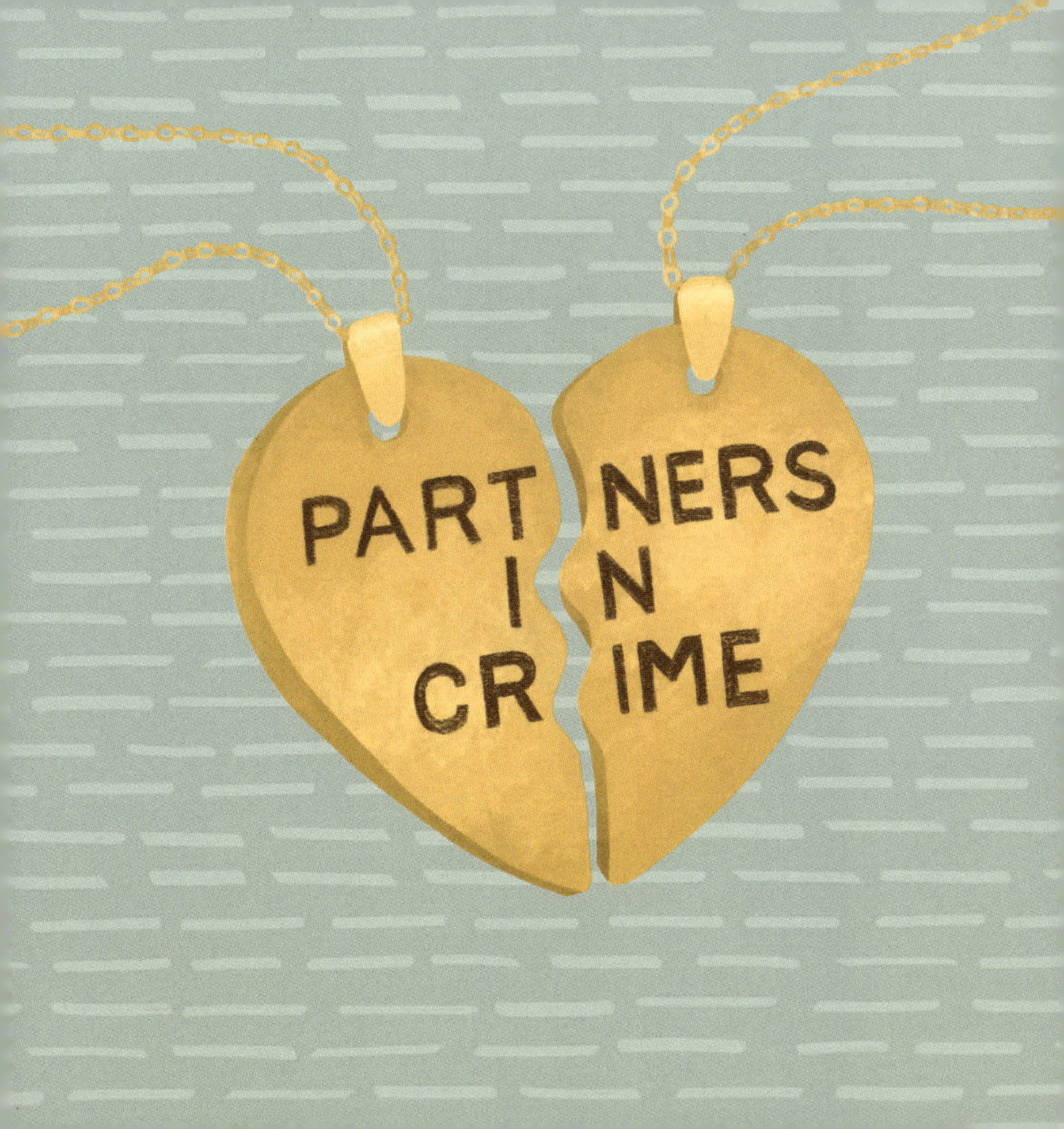
PARTNERS
IN
CRIME

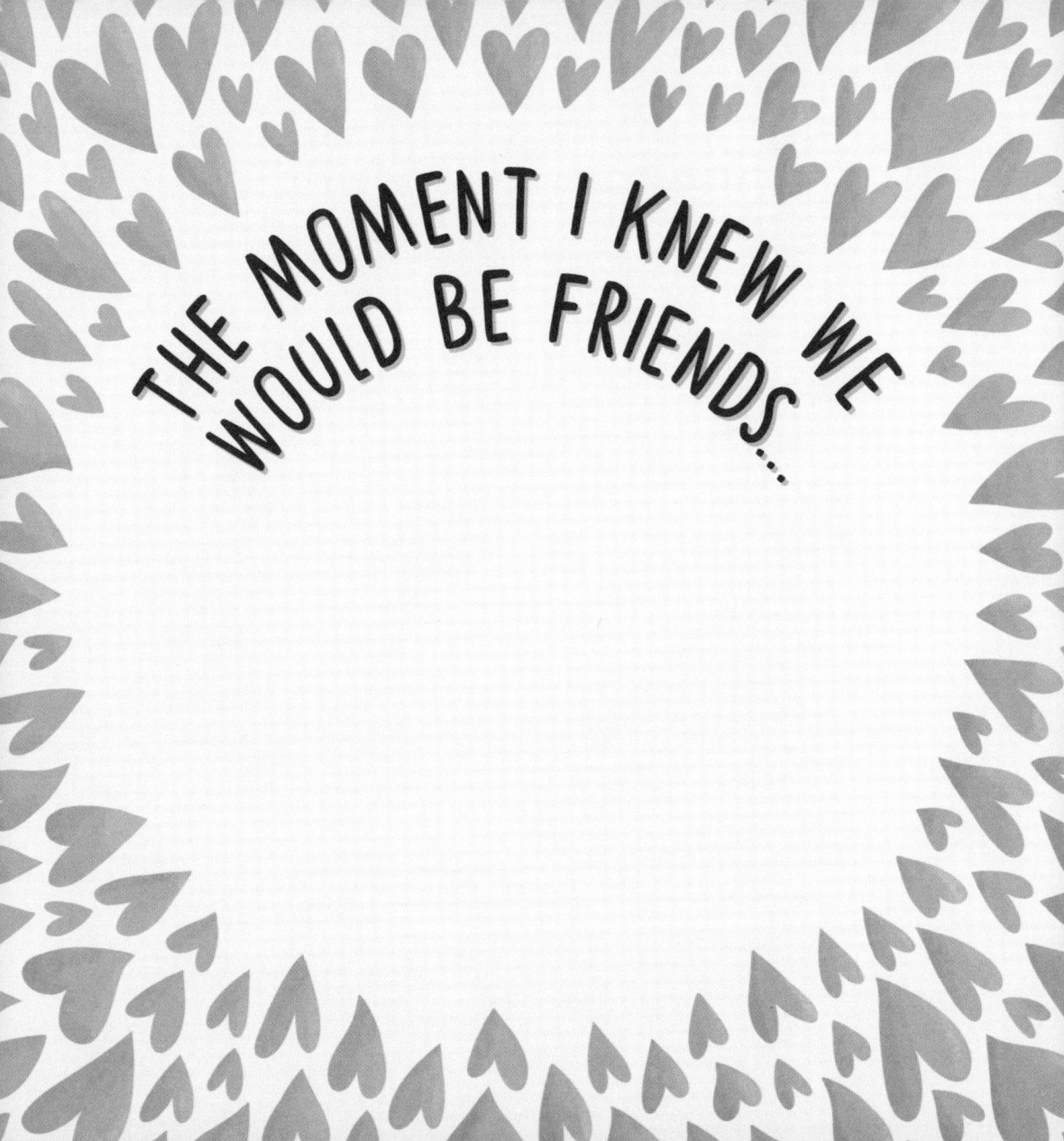

SOMETHING I WANT TO DO WITH YOU IN THE FUTURE...

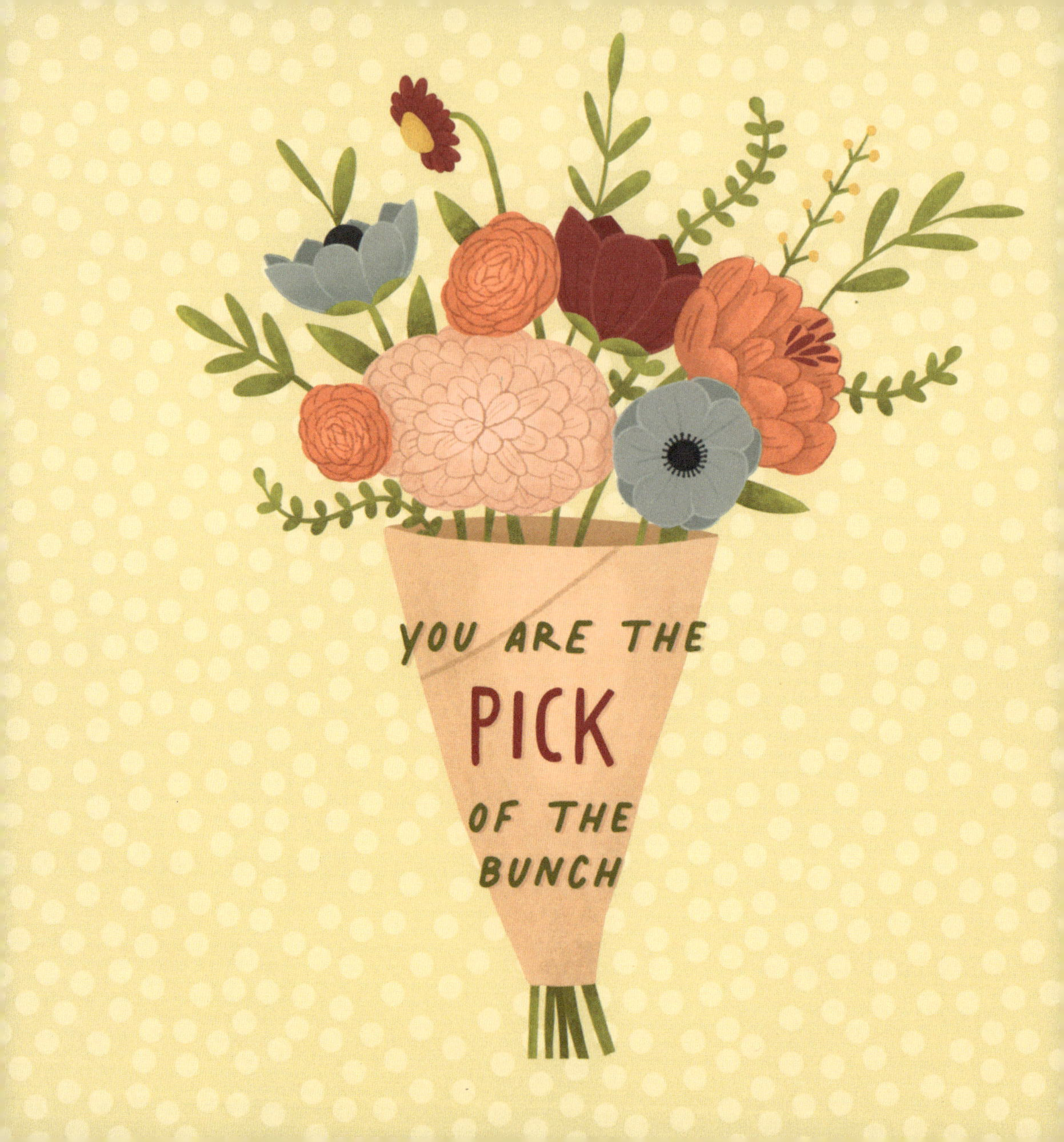
YOU ARE THE
PICK
OF THE
BUNCH

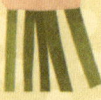

SOMETHING YOU HAVE TAUGHT ME...

TO: you

FROM: me

I CAN ALWAYS RELY ON YOU TO...

IF I COULD GRANT YOU A

MAGIC WISH

IT WOULD BE...

I KNOW THAT I CAN **TRUST YOU**

SOMETHING I'D LIKE TO THANK YOU FOR...

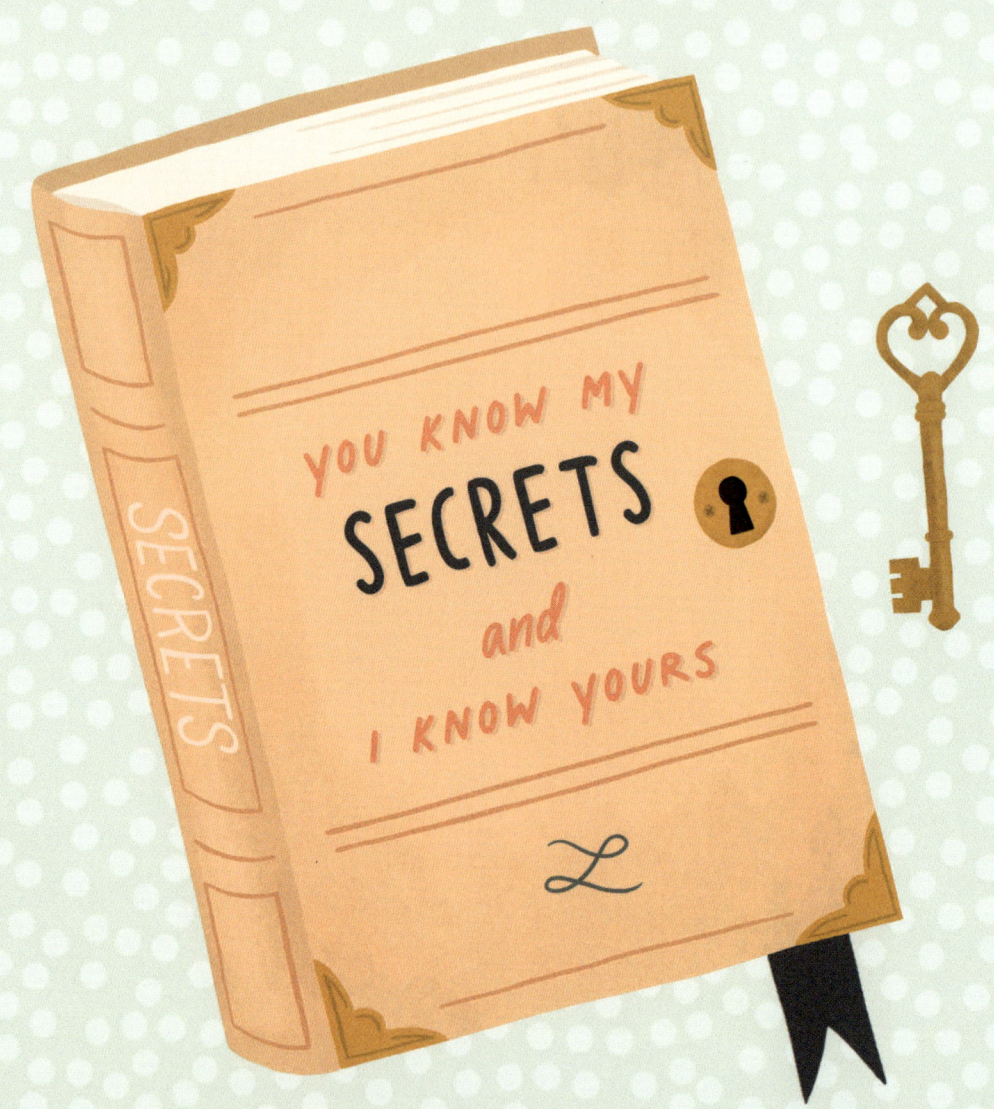

THE BEST THING YOU'VE SAID TO ME...

FROM YOU TO ME

I Made A Book About You, first published by **FROM YOU TO ME LTD** August 2023.

For a full range of all our titles where gifts can also be personalised, please visit

WWW.FROMYOUTOME.COM

FROM YOU TO ME are committed to a sustainable future for our business, our customers and our planet. This book is printed in Shenzhen, China, June 2025 on FSC® certified paper.

All rights reserved. No part of this publication may be reproduced, stored in a retrieval system, or transmitted in any form or by any means electronic, mechanical, photocopying, recording, or otherwise, without the prior written permission of the copyright owner who can be contacted via the publisher at the above website address.

3 5 7 9 11 13 15 14 12 10 8 6 4 2

Copyright © 2023 **FROM YOU TO ME LTD**

ISBN 978-1-907048-99-9

FROM YOU TO ME, STUDIO 100 THE OLD LEATHER FACTORY, GLOVE FACTORY STUDIOS, HOLT, WILTSHIRE, BA14 6RJ, UK